WITHDRAWN

8-05   15.29

DK Eye Wonder

Pirate

LONDON, NEW YORK, MUNICH,
MELBOURNE, and DELHI

Written and edited by Deborah Lock
Designed by Leah Germann
and Tory Gordon-Harris

Publishing manager Susan Leonard
Managing art editor Clare Shedden
Jacket designer John Dinsdale
Jacket editor Mariza O'Keefe
Jacket copywriter Adam Powley
Picture researcher Sarah Pownall
Illustrator Peter Bull
Production Luca Bazzoli
DTP Designer Almudena Díaz
Consultant Kenneth Kinkor

First American Edition, 2005

Published in the United States by
DK Publishing, Inc.
375 Hudson Street
New York, New York 10014

05 06 07 08 09   10 9 8 7 6 5 4 3 2 1

A Cataloging-in-Publication record for this book
is available from the Library of Congress.

ISBN 0-7566-1167-9

Color reproduction by Colourscan, Singapore
Printed and bound in Italy by L.E.G.O.

Discover more at

www.dk.com

Contents

What is a pirate?

Shiver me timbers! Pirates are sea raiders, attacking other ships and terrorizing coastal towns for booty. But were they really bold adventurers, swashbuckling heroes, or brutal thieves?

The evil pirate Captain Hook—the enemy of Peter Pan

Fictional pirates

There are many stories about pirates and their adventures created in the minds of writers and filmmakers. Even the popular image of what a pirate looks like is mostly made up.

Written accounts

There does exist some reliable written evidence of real pirates and what they did. These include pirates' confessions in trial records, logbooks, and even a diary written by a surgeon who sailed on a pirate ship.

Gold coin from the Whydah

TEYE may be the name of the pirate who wore the ring.

The promise of riches

Piracy was attractive to many for different reasons: a life offering freedom, lawlessness, and equality. But all pirates were lured by the idea that they could become rich quickly.

Pirates dressed in the fashion of the time.

Recovered objects

Artifacts such as bottles, tankards, and brass buckles, found in places where pirates came ashore, have provided clues about what they wore and what they did on land.

Expedition Whydah

In 1984, the shipwreck of the galley *Whydah* was discovered by underwater explorers. Onboard, they found treasure, weapons, and personal possessions. The *Whydah* was a pirate ship belonging to Captain Sam Bellamy that sank in 1717.

Bellamy looted treasure from more than 50 ships.

Shipwreck clues

The findings on the wrecks of pirate ships are slightly different from those found on trading or navy ships. These clues help historians to piece together the truth about pirates.

Where were they?

Throughout history, pirates have been sailing in the seas and oceans around the world. Some groups of pirates have been called by different names.

NORTH AMERICA

Atlantic Ocean

Caribbean Sea

SOUTH AMERICA

Buccaneers

In the 17th century, pirates who raided and stole from treasure ships and settlements around the Caribbean Sea were called buccaneers.

Edward Teach (Blackbeard) was one of the most feared pirates of the Caribbean in the early 18th century.

Pirate words

Freebooter This was another name for a pirate.

Flibustier A French term for a freebooter or plunderer.

Picaroon A word meaning a small-time pirate or slave smuggler, particularly during the 18th century.

Privateers

Some shipowners were given permission by their countries to attack shipping from other countries in wartime. Often they turned to piracy once the war was over.

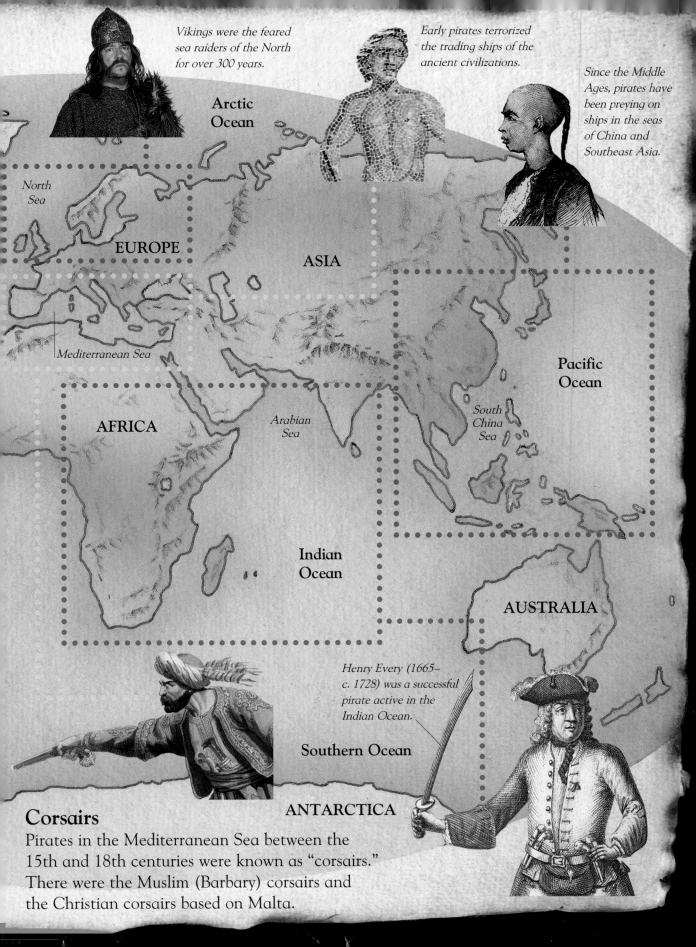

Vikings were the feared sea raiders of the North for over 300 years.

Early pirates terrorized the trading ships of the ancient civilizations.

Since the Middle Ages, pirates have been preying on ships in the seas of China and Southeast Asia.

Arctic Ocean

North Sea

EUROPE

ASIA

Mediterranean Sea

Pacific Ocean

AFRICA

Arabian Sea

South China Sea

Indian Ocean

AUSTRALIA

Henry Every (1665– c. 1728) was a successful pirate active in the Indian Ocean.

Southern Ocean

ANTARCTICA

Corsairs

Pirates in the Mediterranean Sea between the 15th and 18th centuries were known as "corsairs." There were the Muslim (Barbary) corsairs and the Christian corsairs based on Malta.

Early piracy

EUROPE

Mediterranean Sea

Aegean Sea

For more than 2,500 years, pirates have lurked along trading routes ready to attack loaded merchant ships. The early pirates terrorized those sailing around the Mediterranean Sea.

Pirate myths
Stories about pirates, such as those trying to capture a god hoping to ransom him, were based on people's real fear of being kidnapped by them.

Loaded merchant ships were easy targets as they sailed close to the coastline.

Ready to pounce
The many tiny islands and inlets in the Aegean Sea were superb hiding places for pirates. From here, they could wait and watch for passing merchant ships.

Luring targets

The Phoenician merchant ships carried precious cargo such as silver, tin, copper, and amber from cities around the Mediterranean Sea. War galleys tried to protect them from the pirates.

These Phoenician coins, called shekels, were made of silver from Spain.

The sharp ram at the front of the pirate galley crashes into the merchant ship.

Trading ships had broad, rounded hulls for storing cargo. They were slow and powered only by sail.

An ancient Greek drinking bowl showing a pirate galley attacking a Greek trading ship.

Swift attack

Pirates used light, sleek, shallow-bottomed galleys that were powered by oars. These were fast and easy to maneuver, and they could also sail close to the shore.

Growing menace

Pirates of the Roman world sold their stolen cargoes of wheat, wine, olive oil, and kidnapped slaves at local markets for a good price.

Pirate hunter

In 67 BC, a large fleet of Roman warships led by Pompey the Great rounded up the pirates. The Roman army also attacked the pirates' base in Cilicia, Turkey.

9

Raiders of the North

Scandinavia

North Sea

EUROPE

Since ancient times, pirates have also been active in the North Sea. The most ferocious raiders were the Vikings from Scandinavia—Norway, Sweden, Finland, and Denmark.

In battle, a Viking trick was to catch a spear in mid-flight and hurl it back at their opponents.

Broad sword

Arrowhead

Homeland and weapons

Life was tough for the people living in the cold regions of Scandinavia. They lived by fishing, farming, and trading, but they wanted adventure, wealth, and glory in battle.

Helmet

The large rectangular sail picked up the winds on open seas.

Oars were used to row around coasts and up rivers.

Round wooden shield

Sea raiders

The phrase "to go a-viking" means "going on an overseas raid." These fearsome warriors sailed across the North Sea, attacking ships and raiding abbeys and towns in Europe and North America.

The strong keel held the boat together in stormy seas.

The steering oar was fixed to the back of the boat.

Vikings made jewelry from stolen gold.

Longship

Vikings were great shipbuilders. They built very long, narrow ships to carry their warriors for the raids.

The sight of approaching longships would cause panic and fear among the villagers or monks.

Plunder

The Vikings were after the valuable items from abbeys, and jewelry, money, and fine cloth from large towns. They either sold these at a good price in other countries or took them home.

A carving of an animal head, such as a snake or dragon

Viking facts

● Some Viking warriors were called berserkers, as they attacked so fiercely.

● Viking women were taught to use weapons in case they were attacked.

● Vikings used horns as drinking cups.

Barbary corsairs

The holy wars were known as the Crusades.

From the late 11th century, Christians and Muslims fought for control of the Mediterranean Sea and the countries around it. The Muslim sea raiders became known as the Barbary corsairs.

Decorative Muslim tile

Captives' fate

Captured wealthy Christian knights would be held for ransom. The poorer captives were forced to row the Barbary galleys day and night and then sold as slaves.

Muslim galleys

The fast, sleek Barbary ships were powered by huge numbers of slaves. They could only spend a short time at sea, since food and water supplies ran out quickly. The ship's captain, or "rais," navigated the ship.

Each oar was pulled by up to six slaves.

A Barbary galley had one large triangular sail and a slim hull.

Dragut Rais was a feared captain of the Muslim navy.

Sea battles

After a Barbary galley rammed the side of a Christian ship, about 100 janissaries—well-trained Muslim soldiers—stormed aboard and overpowered the crew.

Many Christian ships were easily overcome by the successful attacks of the Barbary corsairs.

Europeans called them the "Barbarossa Brothers" because of their red beards.

Feared brothers

Kheir-ed-Din and Aruj were great Muslim naval heroes in the 1500s. They made their fortunes capturing the Pope's galleys, Spanish warships, and trading ships.

13

The Maltese revenge

In 1530, Malta—an island in the Mediterranean Sea—became the base for the Christian knights defending the sea routes from Barbary control.

Maltese Cross
The eight-pointed cross wor by the knights represented the eight codes they followed, such as "live in truth," "have faith," "love justice," and "be sincere."

Headstrong knights
The armor of these Maltese corsairs was made from heavy metal. They fought with rapiers in one hand and a dagger for defense in the other.

From the raised forecastle, the corsairs jumped down onto the Barbary galleys.

The triangular sails made the galley easier to maneuver.

Helmets were shaped to deflect blows.

Christian corsairs preferred gunfights, while Barbary corsairs liked swordfights.

Christian galleys
The Maltese corsairs had fast, sleek galleys similar to the Muslims', but the boats were powered by two large triangular sails and fewer oars, rowed by captured Muslims. The galleys also had more guns.

Round Italian targe (target) shield with simple engraving

Fortresses
When the knights arrived on Malta, they built fortresses, watch-towers, hospitals, and churches. After the Muslims' attack in 1565, Maltese cities and defenses had to be completely rebuilt.

"Turned Turk"

Some European pirates, such as Sir Francis Verney, joined the Barbary corsairs on their raids to Ireland and Iceland.

Strong Maltese forts protected the harbors.

DECISIVE VICTORY

The last great galley battle was in 1571 at Lepanto, near Greece. The Maltese knights joined a large Christian fleet powered by 50,000 oarsmen and carrying 30,000 soldiers against the powerful Muslim navy. After a four-hour battle, the Muslim navy was defeated with only 40 of their 300 galleys still afloat.

The New World

From 1492, Spanish ships brought back gold and silver treasures stolen from the local people of the "New World"— the Americas. Other countries and pirates began to notice and were eager to share in the prize.

Spain

Atlantic Ocean

Mexico

Peru

Caribbean Sea

Columbus led four voyages to the Caribbean, searching for gold and claiming the land for Spain.

Peru

By the 1500s, the Aztec people controlled much of Mexico and the Incas from Peru were powerful in South America.

The western trade route

Christopher Columbus sailed across the Atlantic Ocean looking for a route to Asia. He landed in the Bahamas and was given amazing gifts by the local people.

Spanish convoys

● Spanish galleons were loaded with treasure in Mexico or Panama and then met at Havana in Cuba for their return trip to Europe.

● Twice a year, up to 100 treasure ships traveled in convoy across the Atlantic.

The Incas used gold for decoration and honoring their gods, and not as money.

The Spanish Main

Further adventurers from Spain sailed west and claimed even more of the American mainland from Mexico to Peru as part of the Spanish empire.

Spanish treasure ships were attacked by pirates during the early stages of their voyages.

Treasure ships

In 1523, the pirate Jean Florin was the first to attack the fully loaded Spanish caravels returning from the Spanish Main. After this, the Spanish organized convoys of larger, well-armed galleons.

Spanish galleons had a crew of 200 men and up to 60 cannons, but were slower than the pirate ships.

Spain

The King and Queen of Spain supported Columbus's trips.

Before 1492, maps did not include the Americas. There was only sea between Africa and Asia.

Columbus' ships were called the Niña, the Pinta, and the Santa María.

Destructive greed

The greedy conquistadors wanted the gold and silver treasures of the Aztecs and the Incas. Their ruthlessness completely destroyed these ancient American civilizations.

The Inca king Atahualpa was ransomed for a room full of gold treasures.

Cortés—friend or foe?

The Spanish conquistador (conqueror) Hernán Cortés was treated like a god by the Aztecs in Mexico. But his Spanish army destroyed their great city.

Aztec treasures were crushed or melted to save space on the Spanish ships.

Privateers

Not all pirates were outlaws. There was one group, called privateers, who were allowed to attack enemy ships. They killed the sailors and stole the treasure to give to their king or queen.

Gold

Saffron

Cinnamon sticks

Turmeric

The Queen's favorite

There were three famous privateers during the reign of Queen Elizabeth I: Thomas Cavendish, John Hawkins, and Sir Francis Drake. The Queen called Drake "her pirate," because he made her very rich.

Friend or foe

Using a telescope, a privateer captain could see the flag of the target ship. He would raise the flag of a friendly nation, so that he could sail close. He would speak through the trumpet to make demands for surrender.

Speaking trumpet

Telescope

PEG-LEGS

If a pirate's leg was badly injured, then it would be cut off by the ship's carpenter. Often the pirate would die, but if he survived, then a piece of wood could be used to replace his missing leg. The French privateer François le Clerc was nicknamed Jambe-de-Bois (Peg-Leg) because of his wooden leg. Some pirates in stories and movies have only one leg.

License to kill

Privateers were given royal letters of permission to attack enemy ships during wartime. But some greedy privateers attacked ships from any country, and kept the treasure.

The *Golden Hind*

In 1580, Drake returned to England on board his small ship the *Golden Hind*. He had successfully sailed around the world, attacking ships along the way. His ship was packed full of exotic spices and stolen treasure.

It took four days to load all of the treasure from one Spanish galleon onto this ship.

Privateer ships were smaller, faster, and easier to maneuver than the Spanish ships.

El Draque

Due to his devastating raids on the ports of the Spanish Main, Drake was greatly feared by the Spanish. They referred to him as El Draque ("the Dragon").

Drake's ship the Pelican was renamed the Golden Hind.

These ships were crowded with extra crewmen to sail any captured ships.

Buccaneers

NORTH AMERICA

Caribbean Islands

SOUTH AMERICA

During the 1600s, many outlaws, escaped slaves, and adventurers went to live in the Caribbean. They formed a group of lawless buccaneers, who attacked trading ships and raided ports.

Origin of their name

The early buccaneers lived peacefully as pig-hunters on the island of Hispaniola. The natives showed them how to build racks, called boucans, for smoking and preserving the meat.

The dried meat and hides were traded to passing ships.

The gold coins were called doubloons.

Pieces of eight

The Spanish turned their silver and gold from the New World into coins, which the buccaneers stole and used as their currency. The silver pieces of eight could be cut into pieces for small change.

Sir Henry Morgan

Between 1663 and 1671, this Welsh captain led large armies of buccaneers on daring, well-planned attacks against Spanish colonies, such as Panama. He was given an English knighthood and made governor of Jamaica.

Bloodthirsty

Some buccaneer captains became infamous for violently torturing and murdering their prisoners. The Frenchman François L'Ollonais, who led the cruelest gang, once cut out the heart of a Spanish prisoner and tore it with his teeth.

Port Royal

The noisy streets of this harbor town on British-controlled Jamaica were filled with swaggering, drunken buccaneers spending their booty. After Morgan's death, it became the place where pirates were tried and hanged. An earthquake destroyed the town in 1692.

Brethren of the coast

In 1630, the Spanish attacked the settlers on Hispaniola. Many of them escaped and became pirates, raiding Spanish treasure ships. The pirates governed themselves, and booty from the raids was shared out fairly.

The Jolly Roger

Ships have always flown flags. Some show which country the ship belongs to; others might show where the ship is headed. But the skull and crossbones of the Jolly Roger meant only one thing—pirates!

A sign from the grave

About 400 years ago, the skull-and-crossbones symbol was used by ordinary people as a sign of death. The pirates took this and other symbols from gravestones, and turned them into threatening flags that would scare other ships' crews.

Around 1700, the skull-and-crossbones symbol first appeared on a pirate's flag.

Surrender or else

The black and white Jolly Roger flag was raised as a warning to surrender without a fight. If the captain of the target ship refused to stop, the pirates would raise a red flag to signal an attack. This would mean a fight to the death.

Changing faces

Every pirate captain had his own flag design, and not all of them used the same symbols. This skull sits on top of crossed swords instead of bones. It belonged to the Caribbean pirate Jack Rackham.

Red for danger

Not all pirates' flags were black—the most fearsome had red flags, which meant that the pirates would show no mercy. It is thought that the flag got the name "Jolly Roger" from the French words *jolie rouge*, meaning "pretty red."

Swords and daggers were shown as symbols of power and a willingness to kill.

Old Roger was also a nickname for the Devil.

Death was also called Old Roger— another reason why the flag was called a Jolly Roger.

A toast to death

Bartholomew Roberts was a very successful pirate who sank over 400 ships off the African and Caribbean coasts. His flag showed him drinking with Death.

Needle and thread

The pirate ship's flag was roughly made. It was either painted, or sewn by the ship's sailmaker or any member of the crew who could use a needle.

STILL FLYING HIGH

Beware—the Jolly Roger is still in use today! It is flown on British Royal Navy submarines returning to port— a tradition started 90 years ago during World War I. The flags were made by the crew of the submarine, celebrating a successful return home. They showed events that happened during their time at sea, such as how many enemy ships were sunk.

The Pirate Round

During the 17th century, European countries began to send large merchant ships to trade with India and China. Many pirates followed them to the Indian Ocean to seek their fortunes.

NORTH AMERICA

The route of the Pirate Round

Atlantic Ocean

Caribbean Sea

SOUTH AMERICA

The Round

Lured by the riches that could be taken from the Indian treasure fleets and European trade ships, pirates from North America sailed thousands of miles to the Indian Ocean and back again with their booty.

The wild, tropical island of Madagascar was a safe place for outlaws to rest.

Pirates' lair

The pirates found an ideal base on the island of Madagascar. There were few people, no laws, and fresh food and water supplies, and the trading ships passed close by.

Repairing

Pirates needed safe beaches to remove the seaweed and barnacles from the bottoms of their ships and repair any holes. This was called careening.

Celebrity pirate
The American pirate Thomas Tew began the Pirate Round. On his return, everyone wanted to hear about his adventures.

Tew was slain by an Asian scimitar (sword), similar to the one shown on his flag, during a raid on an Indian treasure ship.

Arctic Ocean

North Sea

EUROPE

ASIA

From early times, native pirates attacked Arab and Indian ships.

China

Pacific Ocean

Mediterranean Sea

India

AFRICA

Arabian Sea

South China Sea

Indian Ocean

Madagascar

The square-rigged East Indiaman ships were built for long voyages.

AUSTRALIA

Southern Ocean

The East Indiamen
In the large holds of these European merchant ships, gold and silver were carried to Asia. On the return journey, they were laden with fine china from China, or silks, spices, ivory, and tea from India.

Attack!

If a ship's captain refused to surrender to the pursuing pirates, then attack was likely. Cannon fire from the pirates' ship signaled the start of the fight.

Boom!

Upon hitting the wooden sides, a flying cannonball would send a deadly spray of wooden splinters onto the decks. Cannon fire was used to slow down the enemy ship.

This 18th-century cannon is balanced on a circular pivot. Its aim can be raised or lowered by moving the wedge at the back.

Two cannonballs chained together could bring down masts and sails.

A pirate marksman needed calm seas for carefully aiming his musket.

Hand-to-hand

Amid a cloud of gunsmoke, pirates climbed aboard the enemy ship, yelling and threatening. Ruthless and determined, they were well-armed for the fierce hand-to-hand fighting that followed.

A musket ball was wrapped in a patch of cloth.

Patches were kept in patchboxes.

Aim, fire!

Before boarding, a marksman would aim his long musket to kill the steerer of the ship. On boarding, a pirate fired his pistol and then used the hard butt as a club. A musketoon was used when he got close to his victims.

The musketoon was fired from the shoulder.

Sea air sometimes dampened the powder in a pistol, and the gun would misfire with a quiet "flash in the pan."

Pistols were light and easy to carry, but were slow to reload.

Cutthroat cutlass

The short, broad blade of a cutlass was the perfect weapon for fighting on a ship. A longer blade would get tangled in a ship's rigging.

Pirates only had time to fire once from their cannons before boarding.

The spikes of these caltrops, or crowsfeet, thrown on deck could cause terrible injuries.

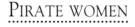

Ramrod for pushing the ball and patch into the barrel.

Ax attack

When attacking a large vessel, pirates used their axes to help climb the ship's wooden sides. Once on deck, the axes were used to cut through the ropes holding up the sails.

Dangerous daggers!

Pirates often had daggers tucked away under their clothes for a surprise attack. These small, deadly weapons were also ideal for use on the lower decks, where there was no space to swing a sword.

The sharp blade of an ax could cut through a rope as thick as a man's arm.

A dagger was kept in a sheath.

Scuttled!

In the 1630s, the pirate David Jones sank a ship he had captured because it was no longer seaworthy. Since then, the term "Davy Jones's locker" refers to anything that has been sent to the sea floor on purpose.

A pirate's life for me

A pirate attack was exciting and dangerous, but during the weeks at sea in between these raids, pirates could become bored and irritable on the crowded ships.

Shipshape

Many crew members were kept busy with the constant need for altering the sails and rigging to keep the ship moving. Other jobs included mending any broken ropes and sails and cleaning their weapons.

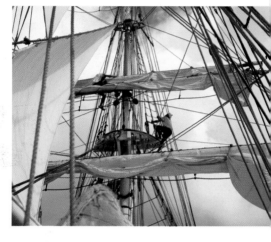

Pirates ate the tough, dried biscuits known as "hard tack" in the dark to avoid seeing the weevils on them.

There was little variety or nutrition in the diet of the pirates.

Food and drink

Hens were often kept onboard to provide fresh eggs and meat. Fish were also caught. In the Caribbean, turtles were caught and stored on board. Fresh water quickly became undrinkable, so food was washed down with beer or wine.

Ship words

Bilge The lowest part of a ship that fills with slimy water.

Block and tackle The pulleys and ropes of the rigging supporting the masts and sails.

Crow's nest A lookout platform near the top of the mast.

Life below decks

As for any seaman, life onboard a pirate ship was cramped, damp, and filthy. Below decks, there was the smell of rotting water, tar, and unwashed bodies. In the dark, pirates dreamed about life on land.

Pieces of eight

Dice

Cards

Yo ho ho . . .

On many pirate ships, gambling for money was not allowed, to prevent fights on board. However, on reaching a port, pirates could spend their booty on having a wild time.

A large barrel was known as a hogshead.

Rats were a nuisance and often ate the food supplies.

. . . and a bottle of rum

Innkeepers welcomed the thirsty pirates into their dockside taverns. Tankards made from pewter or leather were filled and refilled with beer, wine, or even rum. Pirates were often drunk on shore.

31

Marooned

Some pirate crews voted and agreed to obey a code of conduct while on board. However, if a pirate broke the rules, such as stealing from another or deserting the ship during a battle, then as a punishment he would be left behind on a desert island.

Castaway
A pirate left or stranded on a desert island faced loneliness and little hope of escape or rescue. If the island had no fresh water, food, or shelter, then the pirate would die slowly and painfully.

A pistol was useful for warning off wild beasts.

A marooned pirate could only watch helplessly as his pirate ship sailed away.

Code of conduct

Typical pirate rules:
- Everyone has a vote on all important decisions.
- Everyone has an equal share of the fresh food and drink.
- Lights and candles to be put out at eight o'clock at night.

Short supplies

A disgraced pirate would be marooned with only the clothes he wore, a small bottle of water, a pistol or a musket, and a small amount of shot and gunpowder. He would have to find food and drink if he was to survive.

Musket balls

Gunpowder

A bottle filled with one day's supply of water

PIRATE PUNISHMENTS

Some of the worst punishments given to pirates who broke the rules, or to prisoners, included "kiss the gunner's daughter"—bending over one of the ship's guns and being flogged—and execution by shooting or hanging. Stories about prisoners "walking the plank"—being forced off the end of a board into the sea—have been made up.

The real "Crusoe"

The fictional character Robinson Crusoe was based on the true story of Alexander Selkirk. For five years, Selkirk survived on an island before being rescued. He even taught wild cats and goats to dance.

Edward England was an English pirate captain.

Shipwreck

Pirates could also find themselves stranded if their leaky ship ran aground, or if they were too drunk to navigate and their ship crashed into rocks. A passing ship was their only hope of rescue.

Too kind

England's crew voted to maroon their captain because he was treating a prisoner too well. Along with two other crew members, England was left on the island of Mauritius. They built a boat and escaped to Madagascar.

Pirates of the Indian Ocean

Some pirates who sailed to the Indian Ocean to attack shipping were very successful. The stories of the treasure they captured and the fortunes they made have become legendary.

The Red Fort in Delhi, India, was a palace for the Mogul emperors.

The Great Mogul

The emperor of northern India, Aurangzeb, was a religious man and very wealthy. Once a year a fleet of his ships carrying pilgrims and treasure sailed between Surat in India and Mecca.

The "Arch-Pirate"

The pirate captain Henry Every became famous for seizing the largest load of treasure after his brutal capture of the Mogul's ship *Gang-i-Sawai* returning from Mecca.

Sparkling
jewelry

The prize
The precious gems
stolen from Indian ships
were not always easy to
divide equally among
the pirate crews, who
were each given one
share. The captain
received a double share.

Fine silk
material

Large quantities
of gems, such
as rubies

Captain Every's flag
Flying from Every's ship,
the _Fancy_, was a flag
showing a variation on the
skull-and-crossbones design.
The bandanna and earring
have become popular
symbols of pirate
costumes.

Every facts

● Every was also known as
John Avery and Benjamin
Bridgeman.

● In 1694, he led a mutiny and
took over a privateer's ship, and
became a pirate captain.

● It is believed that he lost all
his wealth and died a poor man.

Unlucky pirate

The Great Mogul was furious about Henry Every's brutal attack on his fleet. He threatened to stop trading with the British government unless they acted to stop the pirates.

Respectable

Scottish-born William Kidd was a well-respected sea captain and shipowner in New York. In 1695, he was given a royal commission by the British king to hunt down the pirates in the Indian Ocean.

In pirate folklore, it is said that a dead man was left to protect the loot.

Turned traitor

Rather than tracking down the pirates, Kidd and the crew of the *Adventure Galley* attacked merchant ships, including the huge *Quedagh Merchant*, and took the booty.

Many mysteries surround the sites of Kidd's buried gold.

Buried treasure

Kidd buried much of his treasure so that he did not have to admit how much he had stolen. One of the spots was on Gardiner Island, near New York, but this hoard was found.

The gates of Newgate Prison in London, where Kidd was held for over a year before his trial.

Kidd's trial took place at the Old Bailey, London, in May 1701.

Accused

At his trial, Kidd said his crew had forced him to loot the merchant ships. The crew members there denied this, and Kidd was sentenced to hang as a pirate.

Captured

Kidd's actions and failure angered the Mogul emperor further. On his return to New York, Kidd was arrested and sent to prison in England.

Hanged

In 1701, Kidd was hanged at London's Execution Dock. The first rope snapped, so he was hanged on the second attempt. His body was left to hang in chains along the Thames River for years.

It's likely that pirates' maps, where "X marks the spot" of buried treasure, are just a myth.

Punishment

From early times, if pirates were caught and convicted, they faced execution. Privateers were imprisoned in dreadful conditions, with little hope of ever being released.

Gallows words

Jack Ketch A pirate's nickname for the hangman.

Hempen halter The noose that was placed around the pirate's neck at the gallows.

Dance the hempen jig To hang from the end of the hangman's hemp rope.

Life in a cell

Pirates were held in prisons before their trials. These were overcrowded, damp, and very unhealthy places. Prisoners had to pay for candles and food. Richer ones bribed the jailers for a better cell.

Gallows

Most pirates were executed by hanging. Large crowds would gather to watch the event. Pirates' last words were often written down.

Usually, new wooden gallows would be built for each execution.

Before his hanging, a prisoner was measured for his gibbet cage.

38

Under lock and key

While in prison or being shipped to a prison, pirates were held in very heavy metal chains around their wrists and ankles to prevent them from escaping.

Handcuffs and key

Gibbet cage

The bodies of pirates who had been hanged were often put on display as a warning to other seamen. A tight-fitting cage called a gibbet was made to hold the bones in place once the skin had rotted. Some bodies were coated in tar to make them last longer.

A blacksmith made the iron cage.

Floating jails

To make room for more criminals, old ships were turned into floating prisons. Prisoners were held in the damp, stinking holds and fed rotten meat, moldy bread, and stale water. Captured French privateers dreaded the English prison hulks, which they called pontons.

The laundry was hung out to dry.

Soldiers guarded the prison hulks.

Tiny windows allowed little fresh air in or unhealthy air out.

The king of pirates

At the beginning of the 18th century, the Bahamas became the base for a new generation of pirates in the Caribbean. The most terrifying pirate leader at this time was known as Blackbeard.

From this watchtower, the Danes looked out for enemy ships entering the harbor.

Blackbeard's castle

The Skytsbord Tower, built by the Danes in 1679 on the highest point of St. Thomas, one of the US Virgin Islands, has become known as Blackbeard's castle. It is said that he used the tower to look out for trading ships to attack.

Blackbeard facts

● He was an Englishman called Edward Teach, (or Drummond, Thatch, or Tash).

● There are many stories about his evil acts of cruelty.

● His rule of terror as a pirate captain lasted only two years, but he had become a legend.

The devil with an hourglass

From his ship, the *Queen Anne's Revenge*, Blackbeard flew his flag, which meant time was running out for his victims. At the sight of this flag, many of the ships he approached surrendered quickly.

The hemp cord was soaked in a liquid that smolders when lit.

Scary

Before he went into battle, Blackbeard wove hemp cord into his hair and set this alight, and placed smoldering fuses under his hat. He appeared in a thick black cloud of smoke to scare his victims.

He carried six pistols, two swords, and a number of knives. Even his crew feared him.

Medicine raids

In 1718, Blackbeard blockaded the harbor of Charleston, South Carolina. He ransomed a member of the town's council and a child in exchange for a chest of medicines.

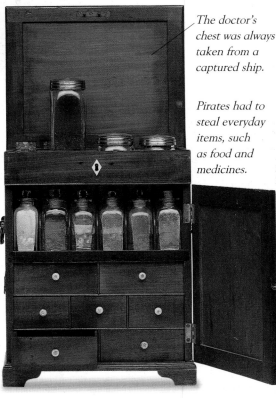

The doctor's chest was always taken from a captured ship.

Pirates had to steal everyday items, such as food and medicines.

Blackbeard's head was hung on the front of Maynard's ship, HMS Pearl.

The end of an era

In 1718, Blackbeard was finally hunted down in the Ocracoke inlet, North Carolina, by the British navy. He was killed in a famous duel with Lieutenant Maynard.

Pirates of the Eastern Seas

ASIA
China
Japan
South China Sea
Strait of Malacca

For over 1,600 years, ruthless pirates have threatened shipping and coastal towns in eastern Asia. They ranged from small tribal groups in light, speedy boats hiding among the mangrove swamps to large, well-armed fleets roaming the coastline.

Junks usually have three masts with four sideways sails.

Older junks had sails made from bamboo matting.

Pirate junks

Armed with 10 to 15 guns, cargo junks were altered to become feared Chinese pirate fighting ships. From the 17th century, powerful pirates had large fleets of junks, and the Chinese and Japanese navy were unable to defeat them.

Colorful flags

The large pirate fleets were split into groups that each had their own colored flag. The pirates worshiped the goddess T'en Hou, who sometimes appeared on their flags.

42

Weapons

eld with
oth hands,
e long blade
ould even
ut through
etal armor.

The Chinese pirates used long, heavy swords for hand-to-hand fighting. Japanese pirates fought with two smaller swords— one in each hand.

BOGEYMAN

European trading ships sailing through the Straits of Malacca were often attacked by the local Bugi pirates. These pirates were ruthless murderers and kidnappers. Back home, sailors told stories about the Bugi men to scare their children, saying "if you're bad, the Bugi man will get you!" Over time, "Bugi man" changed to "bogeyman."

Held for ransom

19th century Chinese pirates sent ransom notes demanding money in return for not attacking shipping, destroying coastal towns, or taking villagers as slaves.

Stamped out

Chui Apoo joined the fleet of the powerful pirate chief Shap'n'gtzai in 1845. However, this large fleet was finally destroyed by British navy gunboats during 1849.

Pirates of today

The threat of an attack by pirates continues today. Some gangs of modern-day pirates use the most up-to-date weapons and technology for their daring raids.

High speed

When ships have to slow down to pass through narrow channels between islands, they are most at risk from a surprise attack from pirates, approaching in high speed motorboats or dinghies.

Many pirates are heavily armed with machine guns, knives, and mortars.

Pirates climb aboard using grappling hooks and ropes, or poles.

Modern piracy

- In 2002, 370 pirate attacks were reported around the world.

- Most attacks occurred in the waters of Indonesia.

- Most ships are attacked while at anchor.

- There were 25 hijackings (or attempted ones) in 2002.

Technology

Some well-organized gangs use radio, radar, and global positioning systems (GPS) to track the ship they have chosen to attack. They steal cargo worth millions of dollars while the ship's crew sleeps.

A global positioning system uses satellites to help people navigate.

The Piracy Reporting Center provides information and investigates pirate attacks around the world.

Aircraft and helicopters watch shipping lanes.

Fighting pirates

Well-equipped special forces and coast guards are trained to patrol the seas and investigate pirate attacks. Ships are encouraged to stay alert and in constant contact by radio.

Training exercises recreate a real raid.

Hijacked

Some pirates take over a ship and create a "phantom ship." They repaint and rename the vessel, make false papers, and then offer to carry a cargo. However, they sail to a different port to sell the cargo themselves.

The cash for port charges and paying the crew would be kept inside a ship's safe.

Safe-breakers

The most common pirate raids are those on merchant ships or luxury yachts. The pirates act quickly to take any money or possessions from those on board and then escape.

Glossary

Here are the meanings of some words that are useful to know when you are learning about pirates.

Artifact an object from the past that provides clues about how people lived.

Bandanna a large colorful handkerchief sometimes tied around the head.

Barnacle a small sea creature that clings to rocks and the bottom of ships.

Blockade to stop ships or supplies from entering a port.

Booty goods that are stolen or taken by violence.

Buccaneer a pirate attacking ships in the Caribbean in the 17th century.

Dividers used for measuring on sea charts.

Caravel a small ship with three sails used by the Spanish and Portuguese in the 15th and early 16th centuries.

Careen to clean and repair a ship on a beach.

Cargo goods carried on a ship.

Commission permission given to a privateer to attack enemy shipping.

Convoy a group of ships sailing together, protected by the navy.

Corsair a pirate active in the Mediterranean Sea between the 15th and 18th centuries.

Cutlass a short sword used by sailors.

Doubloon a Spanish gold coin.

East Indiaman a large sailing ship used for trading between Europe and Asia in the 17th and 18th centuries.

Execution the punishment of being put to death as a criminal.

Galleon a large ship with square sails used by the Spanish in the 16th and 17th centuries.

Galley a ship powered by oars and sails used in the Mediterranean Sea; a ship's kitchen.

Gallows a post-and-beam-structure used for hanging criminals.

Gambling playing a game for money or possessions.

Gibbet an iron frame for displaying criminals who have been hanged.

Gunboat a warship powered by sails and steam, used in the 19th century.

Compass

Hard tack a stale ship's biscuit.

Hijack to take over control of a ship or its cargo by force.

Hold (of a ship) a place for storing goods.

Hull the main frame of a ship.

nfamous well-known for oing bad deeds.

olly Roger a pirate's flag.

unk a ship with sideways ails used in East Asia.

Keel a piece of wood along he center of the bottom f a ship.

Kidnap to take a person y force.

Letters of marque official apers given to privateers.

ongship a Viking's ailing ship.

Maneuver to change the osition of a ship.

Maroon to leave someone n a desert island.

Merchant a person who buys nd sells goods.

Musket a long-barreled gun.

Navigate to plan and guide he course of a ship with he help of charts nd equipment.

Outlaw a person running way from the law.

Pieces of eight a Spanish lver coin that pirates divided nto pieces.

Pistol a light, short-arreled gun.

Plunder to take goods by force; booty.

Privateer a shipowner who is given permission by their country to attack and loot other countries' ships.

Raid a surprise attack to steal goods from a place or a person.

Rais a sea captain of the Barbary corsairs.

Ransom to demand money for the release of a captured person.

Rapier a long, straight sword with a narrow pointed blade.

Rigging the ropes and chains used on a ship to support the masts and sails.

Scuttle to sink a ship on purpose.

Share a part of the loot.

Spices plants that are used to flavor and preserve food.

A navigational instrument for telling time

Surrender to hand over control and possessions to someone else after fighting them.

Tar a thick, dark, sticky substance used to seal and preserve objects against the weather.

Tavern an inn or a place that sells drinks.

Viking a Scandinavian warrior and sea trader of the 8th to 10th centuries.

Pirate navigators used simple instruments.

Index

Acknowledgments

Dorling Kindersley would like to thank:
Sarah Mills for picture library services.

Picture credits

The publisher would like to thank the following for their kind permission to reproduce their photographs:
(Key: a-above; c-center; b-below; l-left; r-right; t-top)

akg-images: 16cra, 16cl, 17car. **Alamy Images:** Paul Gapper 12-13; Hemera Technologies 45br; Trevor Smithers ARPS 30tr. **The Art Archive:** 9br, 37br, 43bl; Dagli Orti (A) 14tc; Private Collection /Eileen Tweedy 36tl. **Corbis:** Blue Lantern Studio 36cr; Bob Krist 6br; Bruce Adams; Eye Ubiquitous 40; Danny Lehman 21tl; Fukuhara, Inc. 3; Historical Picture Archive 17clb; Jim Erickson 16crb; Joel W. Rogers 1, 19; Lindsay Hebberd 34-35b; Nik Wheeler 42; Reuters 17tl, 45c, 48c; Richard T. Nowitz 4cl, 5tl, 30l, 46-47; Sergio Pitamitz 32; Sygma 26-27; Sygma/Cailleux Sebastien 24cl; Ted Spiegel 11; Wolfgang Kaehler 33br. **DK Images:** © Judith Miller /DK /Freeman's 31br; © St Mungo, Glasgow

Museums 12cra; British Museum, London 2tcl, 9tl, 9tr, 9bl, 9tc, 9c, 10tr, 11tcl, 17bcl, 17bcr, 18cal, 20bl, 25br, 31tl; Courtesy of the Board of Trustees of the Royal Armouries 28br; Courtesy of the Musee de Saint-Malo, France 18cb, 18cl, 26bl, 39r; National Maritime Museum, London 10crb, 10bl, 12bc, 14cr, 18tl, 24-25b, 26bc, 28ca, 28cal, 28c, 28crb, 28bl, 28-29t, 28-29cb, 29clb, 29ca, 30cbr, 32-33cr, 33cla, 38cr, 41cra, 42bl, 43c, 43l; Danish National Museum 10cra, 11tl, 11tc; Michel Zebe 17br; Museum of London 30crb, 31ca, 35r; Museum of the Order of St John, London 14bc, 14bcl, 14bl, 14cbl; Rye Town Council 38-39b, 39tl. **Empics Ltd:** EPA European Press Agency 45tc. **Mary Evans Picture Library:** 6cl, 7bl, 12br, 20r, 21tr, 22cl, 37c. **Kevin Fleming Design and Photography:** 8. **Getty Images:** David Hiser 5; JIMIN LAI/AFP 44b; Steve Liss/Time Life Pictures 4bl, 4bc. **Tory Gordon-Harris:** 16bc. **Sonia Halliday Photographs:** 7tc, 8cr. **Lonely Planet Images:** Eoin Clark 15. **Museum Of London:** 37tl, 38tr. © **National Maritime Museum, London:** 4-5c, 7tr, 13b, 18br, 21b, 24bc, 43br. **Peter Newark's Military Pictures:** 6cb, 19tl, 41bl, 41br. **Richard Platt:** 22tl. **Powerstock:** Ross Armstrong 29. **Rex Features:** Everett Collection 4tl. **Topfoto.co.uk:** 2l; 2004 Fotomas 13cl; The British Library /HIP 34tr. **Zefa Visual Media:** Masterfile/Randy Miller 44ca.

All other images © Dorling Kindersley www.dkimages.com